but

This book is a part of a multi-media release entitled *but*.
The multimedia release includes a book, a song, and
a music video with the same title *but* by Keys of Philadelphia.

The song and music video *but* was released by
Keys of Philadelphia and xoMTG
a division of Big Green Machine Group LLC in 2019
The book *but* was published in 2020.

The song, music video, and book *but* by Keys of Philadelphia
is available everywhere wherever books and music are streamed and sold.

The *but see her* clothing collection and the
Keys of Philadelphia merch is available on
www.xomachinethegreen.com

but
keys of philadelphia

BUT
xoMTG is an imprint of Big Green Machine Group LLC
www.xomtg.com

This book was inspired by the song and music video *but*
performed by Keys of Philadelphia and directed by Dana Rice.

but copyright@2019 by Keys of Philadelphia | www.keysofphiladelphia.com
Cover Photography copyright@2020 by Mike Jon | @mikejon3801
Keys of Philadelphia logo designed by Mark Weems @dolothegoat

All rights reserved. No part of this publication may be reproduced, distributed, or transmitted in any form or by any means, including photocopying, recording, or other electronic or mechanical methods, without the prior written permission of the publisher except in the case of brief quotations embodied in reviews and certain other non-commercial uses permitted by copyright law.

DISCLAIMER
While this book might reference true events, some names of individuals, dates, and details have been omitted to protect the privacy of the people involved. The author and publishing company are not responsible for the reader's belief or outlook of a character depicted or an event based on the reader's assumptions from what is shared in this book. Details in this book and this book may not be used as legal use for action toward the author or the publishing company. This work depicts actual events in the life of the author as truthfully as recollection permits and/or can be verified by research.

xoMTG
a division of Big Green Machine Group LLC
4132 E Joppa Road, Suite 110
Baltimore, Maryland 21236

but see her, Keys of Philadelphia, the xoMTG HEART, and the Keys of Philadelphia KEY are registered trademarks of Big Green Machine Group LLC.

Paperback ISBN 978-1-7331769-3-4
eBook ISBN 978-1-7331769-5-8

Library of Congress Control Number: 2019953298

ATTENTION
Schools, Businesses, Book Clubs and Groups: xoMTG offers quantity discounts with bulk purchase for business, educational or promotional use. For more information, contact connect@xomtg.com.

This book is about love
but not the kind of love that enables abuse
or the kind of love that others give up on

This is a book for those who desire to be free
and won't settle for love as they know it
but will fight for the kind of love
that will encourage future generations
to continue in the hope of love

Not because it's forced

Not so we can look like we have it together
but
this is the type of love
that loves to sit in the company of freedom

There is always a *but* in love
without it
we would be lost
in a world where
love is stuck on the outside
and supposedly
only reserved for a few
but
everyone deserves love
everyone deserves to be loved
everyone is made in the image of love
including the *Black Woman*

Love is waiting for us to invite love in
because
love never forces its way

Love patiently waits for us to see that
but
has been there all along

Perhaps we could not see love
because
love starts within

but see her.

Dedicated to my daughters
You have given me the courage to move mountains with
my pen. You've caused me to grow when I wanted to
remain complacent. You are the garden of hope that
surrounds me and reminds me that life is beautiful,
because you are beautiful.

Dedicated to all women
This is for the women who decide that we all deserve
a *but* in our relationships, our history, and our stories.
This is for the women who decide that we are more than
labels, and want more from life than to just "exist" as
objects.

We are human.

We want our voices to be heard, understood and valued.
We cannot, and will not, settle for being mislabeled.
We need to be loved. We must be loved...
the right way.

Dedicated to my husband
Our love is infinite.
You love me as I am. You are my best friend.
You help me to make sense of love.
If I was born in another time and place,
then I know you will find me amid the chaos,
so that love can make sense again.

The Chapters

but war..11

but sex..91

but love..123

but i am a woman...............................189

but
war

but

-sunflowers x roses

I got sick of covering holes in our walls
with sunflowers
and
my suppressed anger led to depression
So,
I decided to do what I should've done my entire life,
kick the walls in

Prison,
the walls gave me a false sense of security
but
I hate walls
I know why the caged bird sings
and I'm sick and tired of singing
the same sick and tired love song
So,
I wrote a new one

Hatred leads to self-hatred
Which breeds more self-hatred
Which breeds babies who hate being here
Which remind us that they didn't ask to be here
and others act like our story wasn't told here
building more walls
to cage us
That system is a pimp

So,
no need for me to dress up mess
and live in a home
where I open my legs
to hundreds of years of
mistaken identity
Knowing who I am now
I can accept no less than a happy ending
So,

but

-sunflowers x roses

I threw out the sunflowers
so we could
build a new home
Everything up to this point
was lost
We lost everything
over
and over
again
in order
to gain
everything

Like Alice Walker
I was in search of my mother's garden
and instead
I found my own
because
our mothers stopped planting gardens
so they could pick up needles
and liquor bottles instead

While enduring trauma
from being in the war on our families,
our dreams were deferred,
hoping we would see life like the Cosby's
but
it never came
We learned to grow out of the concrete
making the struggle beautiful
like 2Pac

My womanish ways
won't allow me to decorate mess any longer
So, here...
Take back your sunflowers
I prefer roses

but

every

          day

we

    have

choices

but

I choose
to accept myself
Even if no one else does

I
accept
me

but

-enough

Yeah, it's yours
because I gave it to you
I gave you permission

You were mistaken
to think
that it was without conditions

You gave me ammunition
to find other ways to define me
since you mishandled
the gift of me

Who'd thought?

Me,
deciding not to be a doormat
deciding to be *woke*
would ruffle the feathers of Patriarchy
so that he would eventually fly away?

You slept on me

'Cuz
my womanish ways
sparked a revolution
that would scream you deserve a *but*
to every woman and girl
who desires to taste and feel
the freedom
that has always been ours since Creation

but

-enough

Who birthed a nation?!
Who broke the concrete with penetration?
Who came out of poverty to make a life for us?
Who birthed your children
even when you and I were unsure about us?

Was it all for nothing?

If it's me you want
then act like it

Words are no longer good enough

but

-options

Yesterday,

After you let me down

Another man offered to do the things for me
you've always wanted to do

With tears in my eyes
I declined

but

i cried like a baby

i faced the hurt

but

I kicked pity in the face
and I told it to go and chill with defeat

'cause
I'm no longer available

but

-make this make sense

if it's confusing
it's not right

if it's not right
it's confusing

love is not
confusing

make this
make sense

but

-better

I deserve better
and
I want that *better* to come from you
I can't change you
but
I want that *better* to come from you

I never imagined me wanting better from you
You were the hope of something better
I don't know what happened
I just know I want better

Out of all of the things we've been through together
I would think that you would be the one
who could give me better

Why can't you do better?

Instead, you make me feel like you want better,
like my best is less
You make me feel *less than*
and at the same time
you make everything better...
Temporarily
until you start making me feel like
you want better again
Like,
I can't do any better

I need to pull *me* together
We've been together so long
that I almost got used to this

but

-better

What did I do to deserve this?

Lies after lies like I'm the dummy
You're here every day
but
you're distant
and I can't believe I dumbed down to this
You keep telling me that all you want is this
but your actions keep telling me you don't want this
Whatever this is

I don't want this

I want what I hoped for when I thought that
this was it
But
this is not what I want

I don't want this

I want all of you
without all of this

I want to know your love is real
and not ever second guess this
I could be the most secure woman in the world
but you make me feel like I'm not cut out for this

Like I'm the worse chick
Like I hold back sex
Like I don't suck your dick
Like I need medicine
Like I make you sick
You make me sick

I deserve better

but

-better

So, fix it
and do better!

And whether *better* comes from you or not
I'm getting better

And I'm going to have *better*

Because
I
Deserve
Better

Can you give me that?

but

If receiving love and acceptance from you
also requires taking your foolishness

Then keep it

but

                                                                    -green

Anyone can come along and stroke your ego
The grass can always appear to be greener
But can she pick out the weeds?
Water you when you're dry and broken?
Is she afraid to cut you when you're too high
Or would she just allow you to die
Yeah I get green with envy
'Cause
What you and I have
Is green for a reason
We grow together in due season
So, if you ever think about another piece of grass
Remember that I'm the reason
Why you're so fresh in the first place
And vice versa
Our bed is green
It's easy for someone to come along
Convinced that all they need to do
Is add some fertilizer to make the grass greener
But
Where was she?
When everything was brown and lifeless?
Planting seeds is not as easy
As watching something grow
Not everyone is willing to stick around
When things seem hopeless
Not everyone is willing to build a greenhouse
But everyone wants to be in the company
Of something
When it's green

but

-here

I can't make you *be here*

Being here

Is more than *being here*

It's being present

And If *being here* is too much

Then I'm not the one for you

Who wants to make someone *be here*?

Not me

I am going to get drunk off of self-love

She can be thirsty

'Cuz I'm not

but

-the glue

        i promised i wouldn't lose myself

but i did

So, since I'm the glue
I did what any glue was supposed to do

        I pulled myself together again

but

i cannot write

i cannot describe the pain

but

-the written ones

Words have always been my refuge
Not the kind of words that betray you
The ones that are only good for speech
The big, bold, flirty words that have no mercy
The ones who will be intimate with your enemies

The spoken word is never monogamous
It insists on being shared with others
Or else it will leave

I prefer the humble words
The words who only like to be seen by a trusted few
The words that like to hide your innermost thoughts
Between the sheets of pages
These words never cheat
These words are loyal
And they are there for you in the darkest of hours
When others have left you
To sort things out on your own

I love these words
The written ones
They are infinite
They remind you how to love again
When the spoken word
Begged you to stay silent
After it slandered you
And forced you to suffer in pain

but

-starting over

how many times do we have to lose it all?

before you to realize

that losing it is not worth it?

but

-R-E-S-P-E-C-T

Right now,
love is in the back seat

Respect demanded to ride shotgun
'cuz tearing me down with your words
caused blood-stained tears that aren't easily forgotten

Dripping on my seeds for me to pull the weeds

Every disregard to my humanity
is a shot to my femininity
and a sucker punch at my heart

I could've fired you
to take away my pain
dismissing you in the power struggle

But
I chose to to take a leave of absence
to love me first

Then, I realized that my proclamation to love me
answered the calls from
other women who also said
Enough is enough

Yelling like Aretha
from the summit of my awakening

Spelling every single letter
like it was the last *B*
that you never called me
but

but

-R-E-S-P-E-C-T

made me feel like you did
by how you regarded me

Like a chorus blowing riffs in the wind
I hear *R-E-S-P-E-C-T*
yelled by every single woman

Taking care of home
just won't do for me
if it has to cost me my sanity

Equality must erect
for you to grow enough balls to love me
then you will take the time to understand me
and not see me how society has defined me to be
and not see me how your family has tainted me to be
and not see me how some so called church folk wrote me off to be
and not see me how some of your so called friends said I should be

Let's turn our backs on patriarchy
and face love
                                      So, we can be what we always hoped to be
                                            or we can no longer be

'Cuz we
cannot be
unhealthy

but

-broken hearts

If I know for a fact
that a relationship is going to give me a broken heart
because that relationship has broken my heart before
then
boundaries must be set

Even if I must distance myself

friends
family
spouse
included

My heart should be guarded at all costs
My life depends on it

but

-boundaries

Real love has boundaries
Without them,
there's no respect
And love,
without respect
is not love

but

-too much to bear

We realized
that were both carrying trauma
from previous relationships
and our childhoods

It created too much static

In order for us to move forward,
we had to let the past go

But,
in order to let the past go
we had to face it

but

-a new normal
(a previous relationship)

i've forgiven you
and these days
the memories of what you did
aren't at the forefront of my mind
how you continued to spread my legs open
even though I asked you to stop
and you couldn't resist proving to yourself that
you were the man

even though I was pregnant
you maliciously told me
that you never wanted to be with me
and how fat I was going to be
and how you always had a Plan B
and I realized it was too late
for me to escape what was to come
when I tried to leave the night before
and you threw my stuff on the floor
did you know you were going to rape me then?

the next morning caused me
to have years of mournings
you took years from me
robbed me of my sexiness,
my heart
and my womanish ways
and today
i'm taking it back

in that moment
you had power over me
for years,

but

>*-a new normal*
>*(a previous relationship)*

the memories tried to control me
you might have left a scar
but I've healed marvelously

and you know what?
you tried to deposit so much hate
but
what you did made me stronger
your little power surge was only temporary
and to the contrary,
i came back stronger

for all of the women who are taking back their power
after being raped

We are living
Breathing examples
Of what it looks like to fly
After being caged for way too long
We got tired of short-circuiting due to past trauma
We got sick of being stuck

And,
It is our right to stand up
To the one who caused us to malfunction
And demand
A new normal

but

-no one showed up

when you're raped
a piece of you dies
except
no one shows up to the funeral
you grieve alone
sometimes in denial
because
life goes on while you feel stuck
and no one took to the time
to acknowledge your humanity
when your rapist took the time
to rob you of it
and then
you realize
that part of the human condition
is knowing how alive you can be
in the midst of a storm
because
you decided to fight
when you didn't think
you were strong enough
to survive it all

but

-do you know?
(a previous relationship)

Do you know what it's like
To hug the justice system?
To be seconds away
From getting arrested?
When you were in the midst
Of experiencing your greatest success?

Do you know what it's like
For someone to hold you up by your neck
In front of your child,
Only to have the police question you
As though you're the one
Who was the abuser?

Do you know what's its like
To have the police
Threaten to take your child away
When you're the one
Who called them in the first place?
To cry out to God
Like a mother
Mourning the death of her child
Until they decide
Not to take your child away?
Do you know what it's like
To spend 13 years of your life
Finding your way past trauma
While the rest of the world
Wondered where you went?

Do you know what it's like
To give up on yourself
And to have people give up on you

but

-do you know?
(a previous relationship)

So you're forced to find yourself
And lose some so called family and friends?

Do you know what it's like
To be seconds away
From being a walking statistic
To be judged based off of color of your skin?
To be misjudged
As an angry black woman
When all you were trying to do
Was be happy and live your life?

Do you know what it's like
To have to fight for your happiness?
Do you know?
Do you know what it's like
To have to fight for your reputation?
Do you know what it's like
To hug yourself
When others suggest that
You're unlovable?

Do you know?
Do you know what it's like
To have to fight for your sanity?
Do you know?
Do you really know?

Do you know what it's like
To fight to reclaim your voice?
Do you know what it's like
To box with fear to get to success again?

but

> *-do you know?*
> *(a previous relationship)*

But
This time
You're celebrating the fact
That you have enough strength to fight?

Do you know what it's like to push?
Do you?
To push until you give birth to a new life
Where trauma has no hold on you?

Do you know?
Do you know?
Do you know?

I do,

                                    so hold on

but

-music is our therapy

Music has been our therapy
Before we could see a therapist
Mikes Davis
Donnie Hathaway
Motown
Biggie
Tupac
A Tribe Called Quest
Lauryn Hill
Common
Aretha Franklin
Janet Jackson
Lizzo
Meek Mills
Solange
A Boogie Wit Da Hoodie
Roddy Richh
Moneybagg Yo
Kanye West
Rihanna
Frank Ocean
Summer Walker
SiR
Mos Def
Wu-Tang Clan
Mary J. Blige
Sade
Ella Fitzgerald
Michael Jackson
James Brown
Jill Scott
Nina Simone
Helped us to retell our stories
When our stories didn't matter as much to them
But

but

-therapy

They meant everything
To us

Music may have been our therapy
But
Nothing can replace
Seeing a therapist

Music might've help me to acknowledge the pain
But a therapist helped me to process it

but

-i never got a chance to tell you

i thought the trauma from being raped
would never go away

i thought that the pain would continue to seep
like blood from a fresh open wound

in therapy
i learned that one day
the memory might not fully go away

but

there would come a moment in my life
where the wound would look like a faded scar

but

it wouldn't hurt anymore
and at times
i might still see the scar

but

it wouldn't be the center of my attention

my therapist was right
i never got the chance to tell her thank you
for giving me the hope I needed

to see life
on the other side
of *but*

but

-faith

at first
i couldn't see past the pain
but
kind words from strangers
gave me the faith I needed

to live
and love
again

but

-the light

when it was dark
i didn't see a silver lining
i know what it feels like to look for the light
only to find more darkness
but
in the darkness is where I found
the Light
it was there
even though I couldn't perceive it
sometimes we have to change our perception
so that
we see the Light in darkness
even when
seemingly
it is not there

but
the Light
is always
there

but

-we must carry the truth

When we experience trauma
And life goes on without us
And people go on without us
And friends
Who we thought were friends
Go on without us
We must go on
And we must not take anything with us
But the truth

Trauma exposes the truth
We must carry the truth
As we walk away from trauma
We must move forward
Or else we choose to live a lie

More lies breed more trauma
But the truth gives birth to life
We must demand to live again
So we can live to tell the truth
And the truth is,

Love
Never
Fails

but

-mourning

we have to mourn
we must realize that the people who fail us
are incapable of giving us what we need
we have to lower our expectations
and walk away
we must let go
and realize those around us
who have been placed there
to remind us that love is real

when we hold onto those who are incapable
of loving us how we need to be loved
we experience double trauma

let go

and letting go
doesn't mean we don't love them
it means that we love ourselves more

it means we no longer desire to be broken
love does not hurt

love heals
love restores
love protects
love mourns
with us

until our mournings
turn to laughter

but

-protect your heart

The powerful thing about healing is that you don't know what you can recover from unless you've bounced back from the unimaginable. You also remember the pain associated with the healing process and you learn to protect your heart at all costs. Even if that means cutting people off.

but

-sometimes

When you process trauma
you need to get to the root
of your current heartbreaks

Sometimes you decide
to make adjustments in you current situations
Sometimes you decide
that you dont want to be in your current situation
at all

You can only see clearly
when the fogginess of past trauma
has subsided

Then,
maybe,
You can see
which way you want to go

but

-RUN

The process of becoming free
sometimes exposes others who aren't free

They might look free
but
they aren't

They may hate you
because you remind them of their bondage
and they may admire you
because you are showing them
that being free is near

Some people are comfortable
with a life prison sentence
living in such a way
where hope no longer exists
but
anyone who despises you for exposing the truth
and doesn't want you to live your truth
is a liar and they are deceived

Run from them
just like you're running toward the sound of liberation
and if they are supposed to catch up with you
then they will be with you

but

you

must

run

but

even freedom has boundaries

but

-*suffering*

I was never required to *take it*

We were not created to live in suffering
We were created to live in love

Suffering is what we are supposed to overcome
Suffering was never supposed to be our lifestyle

but

-the truth

I've found that
my freedom
depended on
my willingness to accept
the truth

but

-for good

We could leave each other at our worse

But

If we can be here for the worse
Then we can be here for good

but

-dirty laundry

sometimes
it's not about airing the dirty laundry

sometimes
you get tired of smelling the funk

so
you will do whatever it takes to get rid of it
even if it means exposing
the lies that rotted into maggots
lies so traumatic
that they grew wings
and eventually flew away

sometimes
you decide to fly away too

fresh air
shouldn't be a luxury

neither should
healthy relationships

but

we let each other down

but

we are still here

but

-*pimps*

we fed a system that was set up to pimp us

once we starved it
we ate

once we tasted life without it
we were free

we risked everything to sit at the table
just to find out that we didn't even like the food

no
good
pimps

but

-live the dream

It is not enough for us to become martyrs
and crucify our dreams
for the sake of our children's success

We must live in the possibilities of the dream
We must turn the impossible into the possible
We must become the dream

Then

Our children will know what it's like to be alive
and they won't be tempted
to let the dream die in the face of adversity

When you've tasted freedom
then you're willing to fight for it

There is something redemptive about the fight

Our willingness to live
when everything around us
tempts us to be hopeless
becomes our children's immunity to defeat

but

-the past

We are trying to love each other
While sifting through our childhood traumas
Sometimes we fail
Sometimes we falsely remind each other of the ones
Who hurt us the most
Real love,
We hope,
Will bring us together over and over again

Only time will tell

That's the scary part

There's peace in not worrying about tomorrow

Is there trauma today?
Living in the past can kill us
We can do better
Let's live the hell out of today

but

-wins x losses

Time and time again
I almost gave up on you
I almost gave up on us
But I've always hated the idea of losing
Unless losing was required for me to win
We have a way of winning together
We have a way of losing together
It's amazing how we stick together
With heavy hearts
Relentless like Meek Mill
We have
Wins and losses
But
It's in our DNA not to quit

Let's try this again

Overtime

You hate losing
So do I

but

-don't ask us how we are doing

The ones who say
She's not good enough for you.
Are the same ones who want to know
How is everyone doing?

The ones who say
He's not good enough for you.
Are the same ones who want to know
How is everyone doing?

The same ones who choose
to selectively deal with us
Are the same ones who want to know
How is everyone doing?

The same ones who offer acceptance
to some of our family
but not all of our family
Are the same ones who want to know
How is everyone doing?

The same ones who say
they have our best interest in mind
but talk behind our backs
Are the same ones who have placed us in harm's way

Stop asking us how we are doing

but

-comparison

comparison
comparison
comparison

comparison
compares
but
comparison
does not
compare
to love

it kills the dream

but

-*views*

I'm tired of allowing other people's opinions
rob me of my peace

It distorts my love life

It gives me a false view
of what love is supposed to be

but

-intentions

A person who tries
to maintain a relationship with
your children,
your spouse,
your family
in spite of their
rejection of you
is a liar and a deceiver

That
Person

does
not
have
good
intentions

Cut
Them
Off

but

-rejection is rejection

Subtle rejection is the most vicious kind
It is when they are selective in how they deal with you
But
They still deal with you
It is when they seem to tolerate you
But
They don't cut you off
It is when they cut you off
But still interact with your closest family and friends
It is when they want to be in your life
But
They have already summed up your life as a failure
It is when they are around
Only to validate their negative assumptions about you
Subtle rejection is lethal
It it is rejection at its best
People who really have your best interest in mind
Who want to see you win
Are those who accept 100% of you
But
People cannot fully accept you
Unless they've taken the time
To fully accept themselves
Because
Rejecting others
Even in the most subtle way
Is heartbreaking
And the ones rejecting you
Are the ones who
Have never really dealt with
The rejection issues
Within themselves

but

-them

If we can persist

In the absence of a like
In the company of defeat

If we can persist

When no one is cheering
But everyone is watching
And your enemies are spreading lies

Then we won

        It was never about them anyway

but

-i am enough

i'm tired of living for other people

i'm tired of allowing other people's opinions
and their rejection of my truth
to define who i am

i'm tired of letting society determine my worth as a woman

i'm tired of friends
who i thought were friends

i'm tired of family
who i thought was family

i'm tired of the church
who i thought was the church

if you don't like who i am
that's not my problem

I AM

and that is more than enough

but

-breaking free from people

I realize
I've got to be free
For once in my life
Free from other people's opinion of me
Free from insecurities
Free from fears
Free from systematic agendas
That disregard my freedom
Free from
You will be free once you become this
Or
You will be free once you do this
But
How I can be free now?
Right now
Free from my past
Free in my present
Free in my future
Free in my mind
Free in my heart
Free in my spirit
Free in my soul
Free
I must know who I am
For once and for all
And those who agree
That I deserve to be free
Belong here
And those who are offended by my freedom
Don't belong here
Because
Anyone good for me
Is never offended by my freedom

but

-breaking free from people

And
The moment I realize that I am uncomfortable
In my freedom
Is the moment
I realize that
I am free
Even baby birds
Don't realize they can fly
Until they are faced with hitting the ground
Desperate to survive
So,
I realize
I must stop asking for permission to live
And just live
How else will I learn to fly?

but

*If we don't stand up to our bullies,
then become just like them.*
-Dr. Cheryl J. Sanders

but

-words are weapons

words are weapons
they have endless power

and with that power
i choose to bring life or death to any situation

i choose to bring life

my words are a manifestation of the energy i carry

so at times
i must be quiet

and at other times
i must speak up

but

we stood up to our bullies

but

we must overcome every enemy with love
and sometimes love means separation

but

-doormat

I am not a doormat

If I allow others to walk over me
then eventually
I will expect others to do the same for me
because I did it

We were not created to endure abuse
        No one should have a broken spirit

Only those trying to regain power
expect others with it
to give it up
and lay like down a doormat

but

-here

Unpeeled layers of trauma
From the war on drugs in the '80s
Tried to strip me from my childhood
It turned parents into enemies
Grandparents into parents
And children into adults
And when Biggie said
things done changed
In the '90s
Our heroes became rappers
And we traded trauma for hip-hop
Here we are
Realizing that our hope for marriage and family
Will be a nightmare
If we don't continue to fight our parent's demons
So, we used books to gain freedom
And songs when we didn't have access to books
And found that the truth wasn't the truth
So, we are glad to be maladjusted
Still proving our humanity
So, we persist
To remain together in our families
Switching roles when needed
And ignoring the roles they try to hand to us
Because being a doormat
For the sake of society and religion is ungodly
So,
We are here
And that is what matters the most
      Because we had to go through hell to be present

but

-here

Day by day
We make it

but

-every day I make it

My first broken heart came from my parents
and their unwillingness to face their imperfections

Instead of facing themselves
they rejected me
just like the generation before them
rejected them

I reminded them of their mistakes
I longed for their acceptance my entire life

I stopped waiting
and I learned to love me instead
but the void in my heart
sometimes reminds me of their rejection

So, here I am
raising my family

And figuring things out on my own
only made me stronger

It is not because I am the strongest
but
it is because
I chose to live
through my weakest moments

but

-elders

The greatest thing
I respect about my elders
is
they did not quit

They might go to their graves
with the deepest
and
darkest of secrets

but

They didn't allow their secrets to kill them
when going to therapy was taboo

They kept going in hope
that we might keep going too

And we did
because of them

Except
we stopped along the way
facing deep dark secrets
taking a break to process the pain
but
we also
did not quit

but

-we should be free

we were still dealing with the remnants of our parents
and the evils that we were trying to overcome

we moved away
but that did not end the suffering

we had to go back and look evil in its face and say
it's over and it's done

we needed to overcome the suffering
so we could move forward without the pain

otherwise
our memories without the truth
would haunt us

everyone deserves to be free

but

-dream

Our parents' generation
swept things under the rug
and left us to deal with the dust

They've suffered enough

We know
because we watched them
struggle since their youth

And our grandparents were our parents
And our aunties were our friends
And sometimes our parents

Silently they endured the unbearable
and left us to bear the dream deferred

Our generation's contributions might be delayed
but necessary for the health of the generations to come

We chose to suffer as we gave birth to our dreams

Without the dream
we all die

We know all too well
because
we watched our parents
suffocate in their hopelessness

                                    We
                                  Must
                                  Dream

but

-the block

The block was where the lies started
We lost our identity on the block
We lost our families on the block
We lost us
But then
We found us somewhere between
Marvin Gaye and Sam Cooke
Martin Luther King Jr and Malcolm X
Alice Walker and Shirley Chisholm
Tupac Shakur and Biggie Smalls
Colin Kaepernick and Aretha Franklin
Kendrick Lamar and Chimamanda Ngozi Adichie
Jesus and Allah
Our love grew strong and we had hope again
And when drugs were there to medicate the pain
And when jobs grew scarce
We found ourselves back on the block
We regained our identity on the block
We spit rhymes on the block
We became bosses on the block
And when we lost families on the block
We poured out one on the block
But
Some of us stayed on the block
And
Some of us left the block
And
Some of us got degrees
And
Some of us became entrepreneurs
And
When we rode past the block
Some of us remembered
And
Some of us forgot

but

-the block

And
We watched some
Like Nipsey Hussle
Rebuild the block
And
We were devasted
When we watched him lose his life on the block
Because it reminded us
That it all began on the block
But
The block was never designed to belong to us
Even though
We helped other people
Build generations of dreams
On the block

but

-we are tired

we are tired
we are tired of our men being taken away
we are tired
we are tired of the senseless violence
we are tired
we are tired of the mistaken identities
we are tired
we are tired of mishandled birthing tables
we are tired
we are tired of deferred dreams
we are tired

we will only find rest
when we find us

but

-healing

There is healing in the community
Not only is there hope
But there are solutions
Anxiously waiting for us to meet them there
In the strength of others
Who believe
That it's never too late to win

but

-new skys

Walking away seems easy,
but
when things are cloudy on the inside
you can't really see the sunshine on the outside

Unless
you decide
to walk to places
you've never been

but

-set it off

I got tired of giving purpose to pain

So, I set it on fire
and watched it burn

Perhaps,
others can be inspired by the ashes
and set pain on fire too

but
sex

but

-i am sexual, but i am human

How can I talk about
love
sex
and
intimacy
and not talk about
my past
my convictions
and
my feelings?

My sexuality is not limited
to mere impulses

I am human

I cry
I laugh
and I cum when it's right

but

-naked

Every part of me has been exposed to you
There is no hiding place

Being naked isn't as simple
as taking my clothes off

Undressing my heart and mind
has many layers
and you've been patiently waiting
for me to get through them all

No fear
No clothes

Experiencing intimacy like this
has been worth the wait

We are not fully naked
until we know the parts of us
that no one cares to know

but

I'm convinced
*sigh
The orgasm is sacred

but

-finding us

i love you

and

sexing you is how I find you
in all of the madness

but

-marriage is not a mirage

Sexless marriage
is
like gazing at a pool of water
in a desert

But
you can't jump in

Who wants to hallucinate all day?

but

-guilty pleasures

I apologize

I've been looking for sex between us
to hold the same weight
as previous relationships
where love was always in a deficit
where intimacy was only exchanged during sex

I took for granted
all of the ways
we drew close
and
all of the ways
we made love
without even having sex

but

I
started
having
the
best
sex

When I fell in love with me

but

I am a freak with you

Unapologetically

but

-married sex

Married sex
Is sex on a different level
It's safe to say
This pussy is yours
And that dick is mine
When we sex
We sex
And sex
And continue to sex
Until our oneness is evident

You know my body as if it was yours

And vice versa

but

-nope

Patriarchy
is
a
mood
killer

a cock blocker

Unless
dry
passionless
rough
sex
is your thing

It's definitely not mine

                                      How can I cum unless I am free?

but

-sex and love

Sex is not good
unless our emotions and spirit are intact

Otherwise

Sex becomes a visceral experience
that means absolutely nothing after the release

Yes, I've had great sex
when someone one was selling me the dream

Yes, I've had great sex
when I decided that it was only about the physical

But
perfect sex
is where perfect love is present
and fear is absent

but

-with you

making love
to one person
for the rest of my life

is more
than
enough

as long as that person is you

but

-*still one*

we get lost in the moment
so we can find us

in heaven
still making love

but

Sex with trust reminds me of the best water gun fights

but

I got a phattie just for you
and only you
it reminds you why we decided on forever

remember that

but

-love is stronger than pride

Who knew that the key to great sex
was to go through hell
so we could know what it felt like to touch heaven?

Our greatest pleasure
was realizing
that we could go through hell
and make it out alive

Lust can never compare
to the everlasting effects of love

but

sex without hope is dry

literally

but

for us
sex is not as easy as opening my legs
and getting your penis to stand up

it requires us
to conquer everything
that gets in the way of our happiness

negativity is a cockblocker

but

-thick

he loves my thickness
the roundness of my booty
and the perkiness of my breast
how my hips spread out
into the thickness of my thighs
and how my thighs
hug his thickness
and my midsection reminds him
of the labor of love
that birthed three children
and I never have to question
if my thickness is too much

but

-on and on

becoming one
becoming one
becoming one
becoming one
becoming one
becoming one
becoming one
becoming one
becoming one
becoming one
becoming one
becoming one
becoming one
becoming one
becoming one

is an ongoing process

        before

                and after
                sex

but

when I wrap my legs around you
it's clear
anyone before you was a mistake
i was destined to make love to you

and only you

but

-exhale

i lost my breath for a moment

and then

you gave it right back

but

-spiritual

making love is spiritual

sex is spiritual

f*cking is spiritual

but

I was never scared of the dick

*-thanks to Lil' Kim
circa 1996*

but

-sex, love and intimacy

God
without spirituality
Is not God

Religion
without love
Is not religion

Faith
without compassion
Is not faith

Love
without connection
Is not love

Sex
without empathy
Is not sex

Intimacy
without understanding
Is not intimacy

but

-*newness*

i've learned to make you cum
in ways
that you never knew existed

vice versa

but

                                Legs open

                                Suicide doors

                                Heart on 100

                                We crashed

                         'Cuz we didn't play it safe

but

-making love

If we can make love
Then we can make love
When the narrative says that
We don't want love
But sex instead

We know we need love

If we can make love
Then we can make love
When the narrative says that
We don't want love
But babies without daddies instead

We know we want love

If we can make love
Then we can make love
When the narrative says that
We don't want love
But money and cars instead

We know we can make love

We know we need love
We know we want love

We know we can make love

but

-the fix

I've learned
having sex without knowing myself
is all smoke and mirrors

sex can never fix me

It is the deepest way for me to show love
to someone else
only after I've learned to love myself

but
love

but

-layers

We had to peel back layers
to get to the love

It's not that love wasn't there

It's just

Loving someone
before getting through the layers
is a surface type of love

but

love
takes
time

but

                                                                        Love

                                                                        Takes

                                                                        Time

                    Love

                       Takes

                         Time

                                                                          Love
                                                                       Takes
                                                                       Time

but

Love
Takes?

but

Love takes time?

Love does not take

Fear takes

Fear takes time

Love gives

Love gives time

but

Love gives time

but

Love gives
Love gives
Love gives
Love gives
Love gives
Love gives
Love gives
Love gives
Love gives
Love gives
Love gives
Love gives
Love gives

but

The love we give
makes living worthwhile

If love takes time
that's not the kind of love
that I want

I want the kind of love
that gives back time

but

love

cannot
will not
has not

fail(ed)

but

-i go hard for you

The society we live in
Makes it mandatory for me
To go hard for you
I go hard for you
We stick together through the thick
And when things go thin
That's when I hold onto you
I go hard for you
Harder than before
Harder than the lies
Harder than the profiling at any moment
Harder than the streets
Harder than your boys
Harder than your imperfections
Harder than what is allotted to us
Harder than your family
We are family
I go hard for you
When the rent is due
We workin'
When we're birthing the dream
We workin'
When we're running the business
We workin'
When we're grinding for the legacy
We workin'
I go hard for you
And at night I make it hard for you
And I ride hard for you
And *we go*
Until I make it soft for you
And I understand you
And I get you so hard
'Cause the struggle is real
And I get you so hard

but

-i go hard for you

'Cause I know they've been trying to break us
And I will continue to do
What no one else can do
Go hard for you

but

-generalizations

relationships should not be generalized

things that work for some people
will not work for others
assumption does work in relationships

there should be a lot of
transparency
humility
and a deep desire to learn

what worked in previous relationships
might not work in the present one
our goal is to relentlessly learn ourselves
and in the process
we can see others more clearly

no one has all of the answers
we learn as we go
we must first accept that we are all different
and then
love one another
despite
our differences

but

-don't lose sight

We must not lose sight of the dream
If the dream is hidden
Then all is lost

How can we love without seeing the dream?

It is the roadmap to glory
A light in the darkness
When all hope seems lost

We must not

We cannot

We will not

Lose sight of the dream

but

-i must carry love

i know what it feels like to pull love
from seemingly empty places

those empty places
where love seemed to fail from the neglect of people
who dropped it there

those empty places
where I felt the ugliest
because I relied on the validation from people
who decided that love
was too much of a burden to bear

those empty places
where I wanted to leave love there too

i couldn't help but to hear
the heartbroken cries from love
the desperate, dire call from love
that insisted that I must pick it up
and carry it

those empty places
housed my deliverance

and I found that love is present in empty places
waiting for the opportunity to create more love
in the barren places where creativity dwells

and I found that love
loves to mold itself into more love
in the midst of the emptiness

but

-i must carry love

those empty places
aren't empty
they are full of love

even if I am the only one
who decides
                    to pick love up

*-for my brother
who helped me
to pick love up*

but

I've endured too much heartbreak

I didn't think I could survive one from you

but

I've learned that our love is real

Even though we fail at times

but

-love is sober

after i processed the pain
i can clearly see
just how much we love one another

pain is blinding
but
temporary

love is sober
but
infinite

but

-hurt

Suffering does not shape me
Love does
It is love who persists to mold me

Sure
Love will give me the strength to endure the pain

But
Love does not hurt

but

-redemption

When you realize
there's nothing redemptive about suffering
but there's redemption in overcoming

Everything changes

Every

Thing

but

-eviction notice

After healing
Pity did not have a place to live

Compassion evicted it
And rightfully so

When it was easier for me to die in hate
Love let me live again

but

-happy endings

We've been taught that everyone wants a happy ending
But
How about we decide to be happy right now
Because life is complicated
And life is untidy
And perhaps
Finding love in relationships
Is realizing that something can be good
Without being perfect

but

-our love story

You know when I'm about to speak before I speak
We don't always need words
Our language is sacred
We are a love story
And our pages
Don't always need words

but

-the taste of freedom

We are not free
unless
we do more than taste freedom
unless
our dreams are no longer dreams
because they are our reality
unless
we realize freedom is not determined
by the size of our bank accounts
but
it is determined by the measure
of the love we pour out when we are full

You see
when we are caged
then love is caged

But
when we are free
then love is free

but

-let freedom ring

It has taken us generations
to experience a love like this

Love likes to live
where it hears the sound
of those who are free

Ringing like a clock tower bell for all to hear

Love cannot
and will not
be contained

but

-sacrifices

Our parent's generation suffered

Their hope
was wrapped up in ensuring our success

They were grateful
just to have the ability to meet our basic needs

That was the *human thing* to do
when everything around them
challenged their humanity

They left us
with a legacy that we are indeed human

Human enough to experience love

In a world
that consistently reminds us
that we are not worthy of love

but

-for every black man

There's a place embedded in my heart
For every black man
For every black struggle
You see
I am the product of a black man's struggle
I am the promise of a black man's commitment
To face the demons that were placed there
By those who feared him
They knew he was the image of love
And he was only demonized
When he could no longer be used for profit
He knows who he is
That is why trauma cannot kill him
It is the trauma that makes him come up
With more ways to adapt
To a world that says
He is never enough
Even though he is the overflow
You see
He never needed ice
Or cars
Or homes
Or status
To show his worth
His melanin was more than enough
His story was more than enough
His ability to survive
What kills most
Is more than enough
His way of loving
In spite of a broken heart,

but

-for every black man

Is more

than

enough

but

-street dreams

my fathers had street dreams
but
he traded them in
for me

-for my dad
i miss you

but

-certainty

sometimes I wonder
but in my wondering
i might wander

thoughts

no more thinking

i need to feel something real
i need the certainty of your love

i'm only human

but

-promise

Something is promising about hope

If you hope long enough,
you will begin to dream about love

If you dream long enough,
you will begin to visualize your dreams

If you visualize long enough,
you will begin to live out what you see

If you live long enough,
you will begin to love

Love is a promise

but

-pick up love

If my religion causes me to hate others
Then I must lose my religion
And pick up love instead

If my religion causes me to hate myself
Then I must lose my religion
And pick up love instead

If my religion allows homophobia, sexism, or racism
Then I must lose my religion
And pick up love instead

If my religion allows me to turn a blind eye to injustice
Then I must lose my religion
And pick up love instead

If my religion sees sex as taboo
Then I must lose my religion
And pick up love instead

If my religion views women as objects
Then I must lose my religion
And pick up love instead

If my religion oppresses me
Then I must lose my religion
And pick up love instead

but

-i am God's reflection of love

If I believe that God condones hate
then I am calling God a liar
because God is love

God cannot be hate
and love at the same time

If I am picking up hate
then I must be losing God
because hate does not come from God

I cannot be a reflection of hate
and love at the same time

but

-emancipation

Love
does
not
bruise

Love
Is
not
suffering

Love
Is
liberating

The taste of emancipation
will give you the power to set boundaries

No matter the cost

but

-a mockery

If it requires you feel rejected
Then
It is not love
It if requires you to be overlooked or ignored
Then
It is not love
If it requires you to feel less than
Then
It is not love
If it requires you to be silent
Instead of standing up for yourself
Then
It is not love
If it requires you to dismiss all of your needs
Then
It is not love
If it requires you to take blows
Physically
Mentally or
Spiritually
Then
It is not love
But
It is
Abuse
Pretending to be love
Love cannot be mocked

but

-losing our way

It is not God's design for love to be absent
from family
from religion
from marriage
from friends
from enemies
from self

but
God gives people free will
and
people don't always make good choices

Sometimes we think we are following God's design

When in fact,
we are only following our own

but

-what u need

Listening to Lalah Hathaway together
we are reminded
that we've been addicted
to each other from the beginning

                God is the glue between us

                                Music is our refuge

And we are a song
that will play
forever

but

-the realization

When you realize that
No one is obligated to feel sorry for you
No one is obligated to care about you
Everyone cannot offer empathy
Everyone cannot see things from your point of view
Every person cannot love you
Some people can't even love themselves
Then
In that moment
You will see that part of loving yourself
Is guarding your heart
And that means
Not putting up with foolishness
From anyone
Including yourself

but

-understanding

With love
We have to understand one another
We have to know when others have limitations

That's when we love regardless

Love and empathy
Must coexist with understanding

but

-balance

We must be hopeful

Hopelessness suffocates love
and produces cynicism

We must be wise

Gullibility puffs up love
and gives way to a broken heart

We must stand in love like a balancing act

Guarding our hearts
hoping for the best at all times

but

-love explodes

Our love gave birth to children
Our children gave us more love to share

Our love cannot be bottled up any longer
It has to explode
Like a well-shaken soda bottle

Love is not meant to be contained

but

It wasn't enough to look the part
We had to do the work
Looking the part can only take you but so far
Social media is temporary
But
Our love is forever

but

-liars

who said that we are incapable of love?
they are liars

we don't care about proving them wrong
sticking together for vain reasons
would only kill us in the end
there's nothing redemptive about suffering
for the sake of glory

it's about survival
it's about having hope
it's about growth
it's about learning to forgive
it's about finishing what we started

sticking together for humble reasons
will only awaken love

there's something redemptive about surviving
the things that tried to kill us

we believed
we did greater things
we are going to places prepared for us
we couldn't clearly see
until now

we know the truth
we know the way
we are alive

but

we've been through hell and we made it

and we are still making it

until we reach forever

but

-the fight

who knew?
you loved me
all along

we just didn't know enough
we didn't understand one another
we didn't have access to generational wealth
and had to break generational curses
to see clearly

we had to be open
to new ways of seeing the world
and each other

we could no longer settle
for what was handed to us

we had to be healthy

mental health
and self-care
could no longer be ignored by our generation

we had to fight
and we are winning

but

-the knowing

we spent the last 11 years
misunderstanding one another

if we could make it that long
not knowing all of the truth

then we can finish what we started
knowing that we can make it

not based off of what we think
but knowing

when all else fails
real love is there

but

-the work

If I want to experience love with another person
then must be willing to fight for it

It requires both people to go
to the difficult places
where no one wants to go
and stay there for a while
even if it's dark
until we both see the light of day

It is not light work
and it's not for the faint at heart
unless
they are willing to faint
from gaining the kind of courage
that only comes from
their eyes being open

but

love is hard.

all the time.

sometimes.

but

-happiness

I am convinced
that I must fight for my happiness
It is not given to the *chosen*
It is set aside for those who are willing
To accept nothing less

Joy is a gift
The enjoyment of happiness is a gift

But happiness,
I must fight for it

but

-our grandparents

I didn't know that it would cost us everything
to get the type of love
that we watched our grandparents share

They made it look easy

Who knew
I would have to give birth to everything
in a sterile environment

Surrogacy wasn't part of the plan

But here we are
gladly giving birth to our ancestor's dreams
before we birth our own

but

-standing up

Part of standing up for each other
Is standing against the things that try to destroy us
Even if those things live inside of us

                                          Love does not enable

but

-parting ways

If me being me
is the cause of us parting ways
then let's part ways

If it requires me to be inauthentic
when we connect
then I prefer to take another way
without you

The way of freedom
does not require me to be fake

It requires me
to be me

Love is never a facade
Love is real

but

-the ugly parts

i love you
after seeing the ugly parts
after seeing poverty replace our dreams
with broken promises and
after i felt like i didn't do my part
after having thoughts of parting ways
only to realize how much we need each other
we learned to give
when we didn't have anything to give
but each other
we learned to love
despite our fickle ways
we didn't give up

but

-fairytales don't exist

I stopped being the woman of your dreams

You stop being my hero

Just so we could realize
that we are perfect for each other

Before we wrestled with each other's imperfections
we were just dreaming

In real life
we are family

together
forever

but

But we never gave up on each other

but

-it all falls down

Sometimes
everything must fall apart
so things can come back together again

Some things are broken
for us to make them whole

It's not over for us

but

-sometimes

The only thing that we've been taught about love
is to provide for one another
However
food
clothes
and shelter
is not all we need to survive

we need affection
we need encouragement
we need friendship

but

-if

If
you do not love all of me
Then
you do not love me at all

but

-i believe in us

To say that I believe in us
means that I'm willing to stay committed
to the parts of us
that we don't always like

You see love
is not selective

It is committed
to every single detail
until the end

but

-loving from empty places

Part of loving yourself is learning that you do an injustice to yourself and others when you try to love from empty places. The model of loving others while running on empty is flawed and defunct. I must take time to care for myself. I must set boundaries with toxic people and places. I must not feel guilty if I am distant from others, because I must remember that I am doing them an injustice by sharing a *me* that is not ready to take on the world just yet. When I begin to love myself, I learn to lower my expectations and love others even if they can't love me how I'd like to be loved. I also know when I've had enough. I must be full of love for myself first, so that I will have something to share with others without being empty when I'm done.

but

-i am learning

i am learning
that there is nothing wrong
with lowering your expectations of people
and setting a boundary with people
who damage your heart

even if that means cutting them off

i am learning
to love people
who have no way of meeting your expectations
giving them room to grow
giving yourself room to grow as well

i am learning
that some love requires distance and space
and sometimes love requires parting ways

i am learning
to love me

but

-i am learning

love should never come from an empty place

the love from within
is far more powerful
than the love from others

just because you don't have a crowd around you
doesn't mean you lack love and when your love overflows
you have reached the peak of love

love like that is everlasting

but

-i am still learning

I've learned that
we see the highlights
of another person's story
but
we don't get to see
all of the dark
and unsure moments
that led up to their glorious days

That's why
it's important to celebrate
the love you experience
never forgetting
that your celebration
just might be
the highlight
of someone else's day

but

-the best thing

The first greatest thing I've done
was to be me

The second greatest thing I've done
was to love me

but
i am
a woman

but see her.

Before black women in America can
become feminists, we must be regarded as
human, first.

Before we can stand up for gender equality
we must be liberated from our oppressive past
that created the narrative that says we are not
human enough
to be
a woman.

but see her.

When will I be able to stop apologizing for being me?

When will humanity be accessible to all?

When will they stop seeing my color first?

When will they stop seeing my gender first?

When will they see

me?

but see her.

-but womanism

womanism helped me
find my voice
when my voice was muted

it freed me from patriarchy
it removed the muzzle
placed over my mouth by false religion
it awakened the woman inside
that society tried to contain

it gave me
the freedom to create
the freedom to love

it called my name in theology
and helped me to discover that Jesus
doesn't turn a blind eye to injustice

it gave me the strength to erect gardens
from underneath the concrete
and silenced my fears in the face of my destiny

it restored my marriage

it gave me new dreams
and clarity in a world where *the black woman*
doesn't always get what she is due

it gave me the strength to move forward

and for that
my heart
says thank you

-for Alice Walker

but see her.

-the color purple

There is something beautiful
about the color purple

the movie
Alice Walker
womanism

It represents our courage to be
in a world that says

We are not
as human

but see her.

We
find
the
means
to
be
courageous
when
all
hope
is
lost

but see her.

-*hold up*

it was never about a power struggle

but

it is
about us having a voice
about us being able to be viewed
and accepted
as human
about us having a place at the table
instead of us *staying in our place*
about us having power over our bodies

about us
it is about us

we've been holding everything together
without the proper recognition for way too long

we
are
the glue

but see her.

-how many?

How
many personas

do I
have to have

as a black
woman?

How many?

but see her.

-timing

There is a time when we must fight
And
There is a time when we must let it go

but see her.

-to the Misappropriated Black Woman

People take from you
And they take your energy with them
By the time you get back
To what was already yours
It's harder
Because
You've been sucked so dry that
It seems like
It was never yours anyway

Unapologetically,
Step out in front
And fully claim what's yours
And don't believe
The lies
That say
The double consciousness
That gives way to
Your ghetto behavior
And
Your classy demeanor
And
Outrageous ideas
And
Colorful personality
Are not worthy

Because,
It's good enough
To replicate

but see her.

-the truth

I am tired of wondering if I am good enough
when the very essence of who I am is good

I
am
good

I was created perfectly

If media is my mirror
then I am programmed to believe that I am flawed
incomplete
and in need of something to fix me

If God is my mirror
then it's in my DNA to believe that I am perfection
and the reflection I see
is a perfect progression of grace
A love story in the making

God is waiting for me to fall in love with me
I am waiting for me to fall in love with me

I am at war with illusions
I am at peace with the truth

but see her.

I am enough

Enough is enough

I

Am

Enough

but see her.

There is a time to pray
There is a time to forgive
There is a time to love

                                            but

There is also a time to stand up for justice
Even if that simply means
Standing up for yourself

but see her.

-i matter

I am human
I am here
I am enough

I have a voice

I need to be loved
I deserve to be loved
I am love

I matter

I want to be heard
I must have a seat at the table

If I don't

I'll just flip the table over
Until it's crystal clear
That I helped build it

but see her.

-blackness is the light

I'm finding
We have the most trauma
In front of the places
Where our purpose is yearning to be born
Where fear
Has forced us to believe
That
We are supposed to be stuck
But yet
We keep producing anyway
Except
We won't recognize
Or accept that
We were born to do
What comes naturally to us
Even if
It's easier
For us to hide our gifts
Instead

for my friend Kali J.

but see her.

-every color of black is beautiful

since we come in different
shapes
sizes
and
shades
then
we must represent
different types of beauty as well
and with all of our colors
and with all of our thickness
and with all of our juiciness
we drip beauty marks everywhere we go
every
color
of black
is so
beautiful

but see her.

-with all of our differences

You are you
I am me
We are we

Why compare?

I will always be me
I can never be you
You will always be you
You can never be me

Why don't
we both
be Beautiful?

but see her.

-wasting energy

comparison is the thief of beauty

God makes everything beautiful

in due time

we miss the time

if we spend our time comparing

but see her.

-no time for fake ones

when another woman checks me in love
i am not offended

her words give life to a dying situation
even if it hurts

when another woman checks me in hate
i am offended

her words kill what's already dying
i want no parts of it

but see her.

-bye bitch

i tried to break free
from being labeled a *bitch*
and the label tried to stick to me like gorilla glue
the moment I decided to be a woman

i was *that bitch*

until I decided that I could no longer tolerate
being anything less than human

until I wanted to be treated fairly
and I was no longer content to just stay in my place

until I decided to stand up for myself

until I decided to flip the tables in the church
because God certainly was not the type of God
to treat women differently
and agree with the notion that women are cursed
and the cause of the fall of all humanity

until I decided
that I could no longer dumb myself down
just to fit in into society's picture of who I am

until I decided that I have desires
and I need to be loved

until I discovered my history
when it was tucked away in the corners of books
pushed to the side like a disobedient child
forced to sit in time out
when it did nothing wrong
and had to constantly deal with abuse

but see her.

-bye bitch

until I looked hip-hop in the face
and challenged it with love
because it gave me a voice
when I was trying to find one
hope when there was none
and courage through lyrics when I had none

but
i'm tired of being called a *bitch* in almost every song

and *that bitch*
I Used to Love Her,
and it was Common
for you to find her and I
together
like birth sisters
and like any good sister
there were times when I would check her
just like a *good bitch* was supposed to

until we grew up
until we could clearly see
that being a *bitch*

meant being okay with accepting the perceptions
of those who hate us
'cause when we decide to be
a mother
a trailblazer
a rapper
a visionary
a leader
a boss
we still
somehow get referred to as a *bitch*

but see her.

-bye bitch

so,
i refuse to allow someone else
to give me a voice

i refuse to succumb to an identity
that ultimately fails to define me

sure,
in my youth
my greatest friends
were regarded as *my bitches*

but
those were coping mechanisms
that helped me sift through the painful truth

when I peeled back the layers
to get to the essence of who *I am*
I got to the core of all women

and since we can turn lead into gold
we took the labels
intended to devalue us
and we made it something worth
being appropriated

but now
we are taking back the power
to choose who we are

and if we decide to be *that bitch*
on any given day
then it's in our power to do so

but,

but see her.

-bye bitch

we cannot
we will not
accept
your

                                    labels

                                                                                     they no longer stick

but see her.

-the real bitch

Trauma is the real bitch
Not us

Black women
Have endured more than we thought
We ever could bear

And they have the nerve
To call us *angry black wome*n

They should have the nerve
To be honest about our history for once
Then maybe
It would be crystal clear
That
It is a miracle that we still have feelings
And that we are
Human enough
To be angry

but see her.

-objects

They are quick to make us objects. They like to put us in our place, but they don't know where to place us since objects can never be called by their proper names. They might label us a *bitch* or a *hoe*, but they have a hard time with publicly proclaiming the beauty of our sexuality and the strength of our outspokenness. You see, we must be objectified to be mistreated, and devalued to be monetized.

but see her.

-who?

I decided
that
all of my womanish ways
weren't mistakes
they were my ticket to freedom

I realized
that
my ways only offended those
who could profit off of my silence
as long as I was minimized
and marginalized
and placed into confinement

As long as I
put aside my *ways*
I was acceptable

As long as my sexiness was profitable
it wasn't deplorable

And as long as my bossiness stayed in the bedroom
I was desirable

But yet
I manage to hold my man down
even if he doesn't deserve it

And if you try to discredit my man
you will definitely hear it

And if someone tries to rise against my children
they will definitely hear it

but see her.

But,
who is standing up
for me?

-who?

but see her.

Every woman deserves a *but*.

Period.

but see her.

and he said,
but you are the real kind
they had to pay to get your curves

but see her.

-my identity

You see
my identity was so wrapped up in men
that I couldn't seem to find myself

I had to awaken to the notion that
I am equal to man
and that the Creation story of humanity
was never intended to be
the starting point for
gender inequality

In fact
the Creation story of humanity
was created to point out our equality

Once I discovered the validity of my humanity
wasn't determined by my race or gender
I was free to be exactly who I was intended to be

Strength
Power
Leadership
Assertiveness
Sexiness

were no longer dirty words
full of taboo when they were attached to me

I am who I am

but see her.

-lightweight?

If this is a man's world
then why do we do all of the heavy lifting?
We lift heavy hearts
We lift crowns for our daughters
when the world knocks them down
We carry swords for our sons
when there wasn't a fair fight
We lift the pride of our spouses
when defeat sucked them dry

And when the world says that we aren't
Human enough to have feelings
Human enough to have insecurities
Human enough to have preferences
Human enough to have a voice
Human enough to be weak
Human enough to be strong
Human enough to die while suffering

We insist that we are more than enough
How else would we have so much to give
without losing ourselves in the process?

We lift the heaviest weights

The ones that cannot be carried
The ones that cannot be seen
but we carry them to freedom
without dropping love in the process

but see her.

-push through sis

Sis, I know you're tired
But
We've been tired
As a matter of fact
We've been sick and tired
Of being sick and tired

Some people would've died on the birthing table
If they had to push this long

So,
We
Must
Push

Rebirth is on the way

but see her.

-the birthing room

There is something to be said
about the women
who will come into the birthing room with you
who will
push when you push
cry when you cry
scream when you scream

Who will
make sure you don't faint
make sure you hang in there
cheering you along the way

There is something to be said
about the women who will be there
when you
birth your dreams
birth your babies
birth your hopes

They are special women

Women who
may have been abandoned
may have been abused
may have been left to fend for themselves
may have been left to die

But
they wouldn't dare see another woman
endure hell
You see,

but see her.

-*the birthing room*

these women
will look *impossible* in the face
and spit on it
to make *impossible*
turn the other way
until
it's *possible*

but see her.

-*it's possible*

We've been
doing the impossible
since before we could remember

                                        this is nothing

and nothing is impossible

but see her.

-Grace

I was there
when you came into the world
fresh out of your mother's womb

She lost 2 liters of blood
while giving birth to you

If you ever question her love for you

If you ever wonder if you have a place in this world

If you ever question your purpose,
then remember your name

Remember that women are willing to do
whatever it takes to bring life into any situation,
even if it means
sacrificing our own

but see her.

-sisters

in the '90s
there was a war on drugs
so
i abandoned you

i left you home
because i thought you found solace there
i left you out
because i didn't realize that you needed me
i thought you found acceptance at home
i had no idea you looked up to me
i guess I did was what done to me

i prayed for you
i wanted a sister
because of my loneliness

but

i left you home
while i sorted out the carelessness of my youth

and in the past
we were barely hanging on
like worn-out thread

and that thread kept braiding itself
until it grew stronger
like a life-saving rope
so we could hold onto one another
for good

so now,

but see her.

-sisters

you're a mother

as you figure out motherhood
i will not abandon you

i remember how desperate i was
trying to sort out motherhood
sometimes hopeless
until i stared in the mirror long enough
to see love in my reflection

love never fails
even though people do

-for Stacey

but see her.

-*to my mother*

I finally understand
Why you loved for better or worse
Something was running through your blood
As a reminder that
Love was not convenient
It secured accommodations
For future generations to experience
In a world where diamond anniversaries
Seemed so distant

Where dreams were deferred
For you to pass down to your children
And the audacity of hope
Sat boldly in your home
As you continuously picked up its pieces

Piece by piece you repaired the dream
And the hope of your children's success
Was a solace reminder
That your labor was never in vain
Although your perfect love story
Wasn't perfect at all
It was complete

In my youth
I used to wonder
Why you didn't choose freedom
As a woman
I understand that your freedom
Had nothing to do with comfort

Comfort was an illusion of freedom

but see her.

-to my mother

It had more to do
With peeling back the layers
From previous generations
That was still shedding
And at the core
Resided real intimacy
Hidden behind lies and idiosyncrasies

And it wasn't until
I loved myself relentlessly
That I could finally understand your ways

It was never about your happiness

It was always about your conviction
That I would be free to love
The way you always wanted to love
Without inherited trauma

I just want to say
thank you

but see her.

-how to raise black daughters

Black men,
do not raise your daughters with
a belt
a loud voice
a harsh stare
or an unsaid notion that she is unworthy

Or else,
she will see you as an oppressor
and she will spend
her entire life wondering what it would be like to be free
because all she knows is knowing what it's like
to live with the enemy

Black men,
do raise your daughters with
a book
a calm voice
a look of complete acceptance
an invitation to friendship
and kind words concerning all women
reassuring her that she must be priceless
because she is going to be a woman too

And she will spend her entire
life dismissing anything that blocks her freedom
including the wrong man

> -for my dad
> who did not believe in giving us beatings
> i turned out okay...

but see her.

-self-acceptance

It's not good enough
to tell my daughters
that they are beautiful

They must experience it
through my self-acceptance

Otherwise
they will grow up lost
trying to find the beauty
that was there all along
buried in my self-inflicted inadequacies

It is impossible
for me to accept my daughters
if I never take the time
to fully accept me

but see her.

-raising daughters

There's so much joy in raising my daughters

Their success in their love relationships
is my redemption

Their acceptance
is my healing

My willingness to admit my flaws
and grow for the better
is their weapon

And to experience them in their glory
was worth every ounce of my suffering

They are my garden of hope

but see her.

-to my daughters and the motherless

Before you decide to spread your legs
Before you decide to go all-in
Before you decide to lose yourself
Your mind
Your goals
Your soul
Your heart
Don't...

Please understand he is not perfect
Please understand he might break your heart
Please understand he might walk away
Please understand he may not know your part
Please understand he might make mistakes
Please understand he might give less than he takes
Please understand he might choose another

And say that you're the one he wants to be his lover

Please remember not to lose yourself
Your worth is not defined by his choices
And if you hear him say *you're not enough*
Ignore those ignorant voices
Say to yourself again and again
I make everything better

Please remember to love yourself
Before loving another
Because how you love yourself
Will dictate what you take from another
Please remember he might treat you like
The queen that you are
And he may even give you his last name
But,

but see her.

-to my daughters and the motherless

Love is a merger
Not an acquisition

Please remember how sexy you are
It's in your DNA to drip
It's in his nature to sit back and stare
And wonder how you'll finesse that dick
And if he doesn't know how to play with your clit
Then take time to show him

And he has to give you more
Than money and cars
He must give you his heart
You are not for sale
There's nothing worse
Than dealing with a heartless man
He will kill who you are

Don't you know who you are?
You're not weak
You are strong
And don't you ever enable him
Don't you dare make excuses for him
'Cause when you open your legs
That brown sugar
Was never meant to be wasted
On undeserving men

Your womb is sacred

Never be afraid
To stand your ground
Ever

but see her.

-to my daughters and the motherless

You deserve to be loved
So stand
Like your life depends on it

Otherwise
You might have children
Who will grow up
And wonder why
You chose him
Over them

but see her.

-words from my oldest daughter

*I admire your body. I watched childbirth videos,
and I don't understand how you went through three of them.
You're so beautiful, mommy.*

but see her.

when you realize
      that you're carrying an entire generation on your back
          whether you gave birth to them or or not
                you become fearless

but see her.

-*every time*

i have spread my legs for undeserving men
seeking acceptance and love
sometimes
i experienced pleasure

i have had an undeserving man
spread my legs for me
sending me to years of therapy
and the wound from my bleeding heart
turned into a faded scar
to remind me that
even though there are evils in this world
love always prevails

i have spread my legs to give birth to babies
who have lived in my womb
as a reminder that
my womb is full of compassion
and
it is through my children
that I've awakened to the beauty of love
in the dawn of rejection
since i was chosen to be a carrier of life

it forced me to face myself

all of my fears
all of my insecurities

all of my beauty
all of my greatness
all of my courage
all of my power

i never realized i had
so,

but see her.

                                                            -*every time*

i willingly gave it away

until i needed to preserve it for my sanity
until i needed to water my daughters with love
until i understood that I release my power

          every time i spread my legs

but see her.

The womb of a woman is holy ground

but see her.

-we got it

we do it
so effortlessly
because
we did it
on our own
we learned to master it
without many options

self-pity is not an option

but see her.

-when they ask us how we did it

We
are doing
what women
have been
doing
all along

but see her.

-Rhea Rhea's song

i never understood
why my grandmother wore red

now I do

she learned to live comfortably in her strength
she was unapologetic
in doing so
she had absolutely
nothing to prove

she was content with her beauty

but see her.

-the color red

        you are strong
        when you can
    maintain your joy
    in the middle of hell
    smiling is a weapon
and so is wearing the color red

but see her.

-for the women who convinced me to wear red

We are unapologetically free

              While some women   look for flaws

      We see the beauty in the process

  We are never a threat

     We are the reason why roses bloom

And why roses add character to homes

but see her.

These days,

I'm not waiting

to go somewhere special

to look my best

I'm going to look my best

so that *special* can come to me

Goodbye, low standards

My confidence says

you have to leave

-To Melissa
& Cafe' Gratitude
in Los Angeles
who affirmed my confidence
when I needed it most
you are purposeful

but see her.

-beauty in the journey

The journey of becoming a woman
Is not to be forsaken
There's beauty in the uncertainty
Beauty in aging
Beauty in finding hope among pain
Beauty in self-acceptance
Beauty in honoring yourself
When others say you're not honorable

It is the journey where I became the woman
I searched for when I was a little girl

And if I had a chance
To tell my younger self,
Then I would tell her:
enjoy the journey
be gentle with yourself
take things one day at a time
live,
even when trials try to kill you
live,
and live life to the fullest

Because becoming a woman
Is no less of a miracle than giving birth
It is figuring out that we are more resilient
Than we ever could conceive

Our strength
Should never be underestimated
Because
Against all odds
We bounce back
We break through barriers
With fine-tooth combs

but see her.

When I
Peel back the layers of womanhood
I am free
To explore my sexuality
I am who I am
Because of who I am
Regardless of who they say I am
And how they try to define me

but see her.

-hold up

what was holding me back
from knowing that i am sexy?

who did i allow to define me?

every woman
and i mean
every woman
is the definition of sexiness
the synonym of strength
and the antonym of defeat

i was never designed to be weak
whoever says so is a liar

it's obvious
like a knock off designer bag

but see her.

-beauty

I've learned that

I am
beautiful

It's not that I wasn't beautiful before
But there's something beautiful about recognizing it

When you recognize it
You truly become it
There's no pretending

It was there all along
Waiting for you to see it

Truly see it for what it is...

                    Acceptance

but see her.

-royalty

our experiences are unique to us
and we still love the colors black and purple
despite the abuse that left scars
as a reminder
that things were never supposed to be this way

the imprint of royalty
couldn't be erased from our DNA

even though
we could have stayed in this place
where there was no means to an end
we come from a lineage that did more
than make ends meet

but see her.

-injustice

I can not
truly stand up
for justice

                                                                      If I'm doing
an injustice to
myself

but see her.

-becoming

accepting myself
was by far
the most important part
of becoming a woman
no one
and i mean
no one
can ever do it for me

but see her.

we don't have to carry it any longer

freedom can carry it

but see her.

-details

There are details about me
that can only be understood
by those who have experienced
what I've experienced
Who agree
that this was never about the conquest for power
but about having an equal place in humanity

It's about holding our loved ones accountable
because we are the only ones who understand
why we behave the way we do

It's about being clothed in strength
without even thinking about it
because that's what we watched our mothers do

It's nothing for us to leave our homes
to go to foreign places
for a better life
because that's what we were always forced to do

We embrace the beauty of who we are
regardless if we have
natural hair
perms
extensions

And our conquest
for a comfortable place in society
was never really about

fancy cars, stock options or pensions

but see her.

-*details*

It was about
securing a future for the next generation
                              because we never got reparations

We have an unsaid understanding
that *checking our men*
was never about having an attitude problem
but
it was about us wanting
to see our men win
in a society
where they are constantly faced with indoctrination

It's about our love for all women
and how we have helped each other
to love ourselves
and survive what kills most
when they tried
to make it seem
as though
we are unlovable

but see her.

-new beginnings

When I was broken
You reminded me that I was the glue

When I was low
The breath from your words made me fly

When my sexiness was offensive
You never slept on me like the others
Cuz
Sometimes
Sexiness is only offensive
Based off of the skin you're in

And if a woman is not woke
She will overlook liberation
For the sake of privilege

When I was lost
You never used my weakness
To justify my unworthiness to others
When I was winning
I saw that you were happy with me

Women who have struggled
Still taste the struggle during the celebration
And the aftertaste of empathy
Won't let them be distasteful
During someone else's new beginnings

Healing happens
In the company of true sisterhood

but see her.

-*words from Kali J.*

We lose our greatness
waiting for the responses of other people

but see her.

-her

I hope you see
the humanity of the *Black Woman*
on every page
and in every word

I hope you see
that her sexuality
is not limited to her sensuality
but
it is the essence
surrounding her sexuality
that makes her sexiness a gift

I hope you see
that if you don't make room for her
she will unapologetically take up space

I hope you see
her anger as justice
and
her tears as a baptism
for those who are thirsty for liberation

I hope you see
that she is love
and she is never wrapped up in validation
but
she is clothed in hope
because
she knows who she is
when others don't

So,

but see her.

-*her*

I hope
before
you see
her

you *see* her

but see her.

Credits:

The term and concept of *womanism* was created by Alice Walker in her book *In Search of Our Mother's Gardens*.

Walker, Alice. In Search of Our Mother's Garden. San Diego: Harcourt Brace Jovanovich, 1983.

The concept of *a rose growing out of the concrete* was first used by Tupac Shakur in his poetry book *The Rose that Grew From Concrete*.

Shakur, Tupac. The Rose That Grew From Concrete. New York: MTV Books/Pocket Books, 1999.

The concept of a *knowing why a caged bird sings* was referenced by Maya Angelou in her book *I Know Why the Caged Bird Sings* and first mentioned by Paul Lawrence Dunbar in his poem *Sympathy*.

Angelou. Maya. I Know Why the Caged Bird Sings. New York: Random House, 2015. (First copywritten and published in 1969)

Wins and Losses is the third studio album and song by Meek Mills released July 21, 2017.

I Used to Love Her is is a hip-hop song by Common released September, 27, 1994.

Stream, watch and purchase our song and music video
but by Keys of Philadelphia

Subscribe and listen to our podcast:
but by Keys of Philadelphia

Watch, listen, like and subscribe
to our family Youtube channel and podcast:
Our Big Green Life

Learn more about our company:
www.xomtg.com
@machinethegreen

Buy our merch and support our clothing line.
We make donations from every sale to our community partners:
www.xomachinethegreen.com
@xomachinethegreen

www.keysofphiladelphia.com
@keysofphiladelphia

www.ingramcontent.com/pod-product-compliance
Lightning Source LLC
Chambersburg PA
CBHW031102080526
44587CB00011B/786